Eat Well
& Get DOTS of Rest

Wolfie's Guide to the Good Life

Wolfie Maine Coon
with Michael McGaulley Editor & food-server

CONTENTS

Foreword
by Tippie MaacCaat

My uncle, Wolfie Maine Coon, was a legend in his own first lifetime.

And after that first lifetime ended, he went on to become St. Wolfie, the Patron Saint of Lost and Homeless Cats. You probably read about that in "The Cat Who Brought Us a Bottle of Wine from the Popes' Private Reserve," in the book CHICKEN SOUP FOR THE CAT-LOVER'S SOUL, which was a huge best-seller because there are so many cat lovers.

That's why I'm here now, sitting in a nice warm home, writing my blog every day -- because St. Wolfie drew me, and my Pop-cat before me, and Elsie and Nellie and Al and Graycie and Sweet-Pea and a whole lot of other cats who needed nice homes.

Back when he was scratching the earth, Wolfie was the King of Whatever Neighborhood he was living in at the time, and even 2-leggeds respected that. For us 4-leggeds, he became our Guide and Patron Saint.

And now, I just found, there was even more to my uncle Wolfie!

Not only was he, at 27 pounds, the biggest cat anybody around there had ever seen.

Not only was he the cat who put the "rest" in Reston, Virginia, where he lived for a while.

Not only was he the cat who pioneered the method that taught the rest of us how to learn to read and write by watching TV commercials and paying attention to the way 2-leggeds hit computers to make words pop up.

Not only all that, but as I found one night when I was pawing through our family computer, Uncle Wolfie had written the first self-help book for cats!

Which you are now holding in your paws!

Uncle Wolfie sure knew how to live, and I hope this book helps you as much as it has helped me!

Tippie MaacCaat is the 97th Great Great Great Grandson of Admiral MaacCaat who sailed with the British fleet to invade America, but then sniffed which way the winds were blowing, and decided to shift loyalties and pursue pursue opportunities in this country.

Follow Tippie's Blog at www.CatSelfHelp.com opportunities in this country.

Follow Tippie's Blog at www.CatSelfHelp.com.

Part One
First Things First: Food

Rule #1

To make sure YOUR breakfast is

EVERY BITE

as good as it should be,

don't let THEM oversleep!

Do WHATEVER IT TAKES

to get them up and moving!

Tip: Hop up on the bed, get real close to their faces, and just stare at them. They will get the point.

Rule #2

Get a jump on the day.

Never, ever be late for breakfast.

Breakfast is the most important meal of your early morning.

If you sleep through it, you'll be playing catch-up all day.

Besides, it's the only meal before dinner-time when your 2-leggeds will be there to dish out extra helpings.

Do not oversleep!

That's my nephew in the picture

They call him Little Red. He oversleeps a lot and misses breakfast, and that is why he is so little and scrawny.

HARD TO BELIEVE! Sometimes Little Red even sleeps through his SECOND breakfast!

Sometimes he doesn't wake up for other meals!

Except at bedtime: Then he's always first to the plate for his bedtime snack!

Rule #3

A Nap after breakfast

Leaves you rested & ready

For Lunch!

Rule #4

Food is love!

The MORE they feed you,

The MORE they love you,

and,

The MORE you eat,

The MORE you

Show your love in return!

SO NEVER LEAVE ANY FOOD ON YOUR PLATE!

Rule #5

It's true! The other plate really IS always tastier!

Don't ask why, it's just one of those things , like when you knock a plant off the window-sill, it always falls downwards. Why? Who knows?

Tip: If your 2-leggeds leave their plates on the table and walk away, then those plates are fair game. Jump up, gobble what you can, then get down before they come back. They probably won't even notice.

Tip: It's bad manners to push your way in to sample another cat's plate, even if you're bigger. It's just not the right thing to do.

Tip: But maybe that other cat is admiring your plate just as you're envying his. If that's the case, just trade places.

My secret trick: sometimes I walk away from my plate, which lures the other cat to move over to sample mine, and then I zip in and take over the plate he (or she) left.

Here I am with my old friend, Puss N. Boots. He drops by every evening just before dinner-time.

He says food always tastes better at my house.

Someday maybe I should visit for dinner at his house.

But it's a pretty long walk.

Rule #6

A day without tuna soup

is like a day without a snooze in the sunshine!

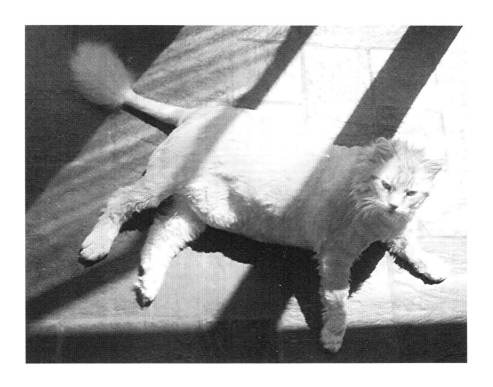

WHAT? You say your people have never made tuna soup for you? Here's my personal recipe.

Wolfie's Tuna Soup

Preparation time: 2 minutes   Number of servings: 1 medium cat

INGREDIENTS	HOW - TO
1 can of PQT (people-quality tuna, such as solid white or at least chunk light) in spring water More spring water, for rinsing	Open the can of tuna. Pour the broth from the can into the cats bowl. Leave the tuna in the can and rinse it ONCE (not more, so as not to dilute the flavor), then pour that rinse-water into the bowl, mixing it thoroughly with the original full-strength broth. Add some pieces of tuna to give the soup body. Serve immediately, then place rest of tuna on cats plate as the main course.

Rule #7

Love your family and friends.

But eat first, socialize later.

Rule #8

I never met a ham I didn't like.

The same goes for chickens and fishes --they're also very likeable.

But they're not the only good things to eat. A lot of us only trust the foods we had as kittens, but there are lots and lots of tasty foods in the world, all worth sampling. If you're open to new flavors, you'll find that some of those new things will become your real favorites.

Smart cats stick close to their 2-leggeds during meal-time, so they're right there, ready for samples.

That's how I got to try scallops for the first time . . . and they tasted so great that I wished I'd found them a lot earlier in this lifetime!

Try everything once.

If you don't like it, then just spit it out.

Rule #9

Even 9 lives are 2 short for cheap cat-food.

Demand nothing but the best, NOW!

This is my pal, Al.

Al likes his ham hand-fed.

He's like me, a guy with a taste for the best.

Rule #10

Hold out! The best is yet to come!

Important tip: No matter how hungry you are, always turn up your nose at the first thing they put in front of you. Sniff it, maybe lick it, BUT DO NOT EAT IT.

Instead, look up at the server with your eyes wide, showing your disbelief and disappointment. Get that look down right, and you'll shame them into giving the good stuff right from the start.

Part Two
Living Smart

Rule #11

Listen and learn. Be an Edu—Cat—ed Cat!

I was taken away from my Momcat before I finished my home-schooling. But I didn't let that hold me back. When I got to my first home, I made up my mind to get an education on my own.

Here's what you really, really need to know:

TIME: Learn breakfast-time, lunch-time, dinner-time, and, of course, bed-time.

NUMBERS: You need to be able to count up to six (that's one more than most of us have toes). One is breakfast, two is mid-morning snack, three is lunch, four is afternoon tea (also known as "4-sies"), five is dinner, and six is bed-time snack. Miss one of those, and your count is thrown off.

2-LEGGED LANGUAGE: I learned it by watching the TV, and taught myself how to read words from the ads. You can do it, too!

But NEVER let on that you understand what they're saying!   Play dumb!

Stay alert! Watch closely! Learn! Tuck it away!

Rule #12

Don't waste energy— take it easy.

Nobody ever had to scold me to not waste energy. That's something I've known ever since I was just a tiny, little kitten — energy is just too precious to waste on useless movement.

Take it easy, rest up between meals, and let things take care of themselves.

I take it easy best on my electrically-heated bed

18

Rule #13

Catnip and catnaps!

Treat yourself often to the joys of life!

My people took this picture the day our cousin in Alaska sent me some special Alaska 'nip.

Once I got a whiff of it, I knew I couldn't wait until Christmas, so I tore open the gift-wrapping and dug in. I want to go to Alaska someday. Wherever that is.

Rule #14

Catnip: never inhale.

My Momcat didn't let us try catnip when we were growing up. She said it would stunt our growth.

Now that I'm older and wiser, I think the truth is that our Popcat had a problem in hitting the 'nip too hard, and she was afraid we'd take after him.

Nonetheless, she did teach us proper catnip etiquette, so we wouldn't embarrass ourselves when we grew up. I'm passing it on to you.

What happens when cats inhale 'nip

Some cats get mean when they inhale. Other cats (like me), get soppy and sentimental and affectionate, and that can be pretty embarrassing.

One time, my people held a catnip party for me and my friends. I inhaled some of it, and next thing there I was reached out and put my arm around my good friend Kitty to show how much I really liked her.

But she slapped my face and jumped up hissing for me to keep my paws to myself. That kind of ruined the mood.

Nowadays, I tend to doze off after a catnip party, sometimes even before the company has gone home.

That's my friend Puss N. Boots hanging around after a 'nip party at my house. He's hoping they'll give him one more for the road.

Did they? I don't know, I was VERY asleep.

MOMCAT'S RULES ON 'NIP CATETIQUETTE

1 First, approach and sniff the weed. Savor the aroma. Perhaps nibble a little — but not too much. Definitely DO NOT INHALE, as that makes a cat very silly.

2 Next, plop onto it with your full body. Roll around, so it gets in your fur.

3 Enjoy.

4 Finally, snoooooooooooze.

5 It's okay to roll in catnip, and it's perfectly fine to lick it, even taste a little.

6 But, as I said, definitely do not inhale, because that's when you lose your feline inhibitions. That can get you into trouble.

Part Three
Your Health and Well-Being

Rule #15

"Let's go for a little ride"

ALWAYS means BAD NEWS!

HIDE!

2-leggeds are sneaky. They use words to trick us.

Suppose your people say, "Let's go for a little ride." Sounds good, doesn't it? You think of a drive in the country, or maybe a trip to the fish-market, followed by a stop for your own bowl of soft ice cream.

Sad to say, things don't work that way!

Most of the time, that "little ride" will be to a place you definitely DO NOT want to go, like a doctors' office, where bad things happen to you, things like needles stuck into you, pills shoved down your throat, and (worst of all) thermometers slid into A VERY PERSONAL PART of your body!

Another nasty "little ride" takes you to what the 2-leggeds call the "Feline Care Salon."

That's where they strap you to a table and then buzz off all the hair you've spent the whole winter growing. Then — I am NOT joking !— they put soap and water all over your body and scrub! They don't know that cats are allergic to water.

Me before haircut

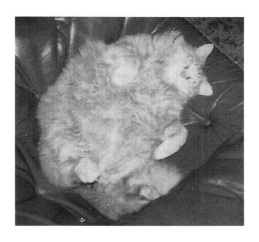

After haircut!

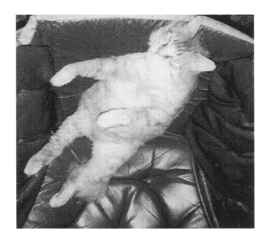

The good side to that first haircut:

I became Famous as the Restin' Lion of Reston!

I was really embarrassed after that first haircut. I felt naked without the fur I'd spent that whole first lifetime growing! I hid for days.

I finally went outside and hid under the bushes. But I got a real surprise: When the 2-leggeds in the neighborhood saw the New Me they made me feel like a star! They had never seen anybody like me!

My Fur Stylist had given what they called "The Lion's Cut." That left me all the hair around my head and on the tip of my tail, and I looked like a little lion, and Mee-oow wow wow!!! let me tell you the 2-leggeds loved that!

They all wanted to rub my back. They said it felt like velvet, whatever velvet is. It felt really nice when they did that, and that's when I got very famous in the town where we lived, which was a place called Reston. I was the one and only Lion of Reston!

I think a Lion's Cut is a very good style for a Maine Coon.

Warning! There are other bad rides

There are other "little rides" to be wary of, like when they say, "We're going on vacation." That sounds great, and you have visions of lying under a palm tree sipping coconut milk.

But it's not "We," it's "They," your 2-leggeds, who are going off to lie in the sun, and you're about to be dumped in some strange place away from all your favorite foods and comfortable resting spots.

In some of those places, you'll be locked in a prison cell, tortured by the sounds of dogs barking all day long!

What to do if you hear them whisper about a "little ride"

1 HIDE! But they'll probably out-wait you and grab you when you come out for a bite to eat.

2 PLAY DIRTY! This IS the time for serious jaws & claws!

3 If all else fails, PUNISH them when you finally get back home. Make their lives miserable for a while, just as they made your life miserable! Maybe "forget" to use the litter box, and make your deposits wherever you please. Or find creative new places to sharpen your claws. Next time, they'll think twice before taking you on that "little ride" to hell!

Rule #16

If you aren't broken,

Don't let them fix you!

I'll say it again, 2-leggeds are sneaky creatures who use words to trick us. "Let's take a little ride" is tricky enough. But the worst trick of all is when they offer to "fix" you.

I was young and naive then, and it sounded like a good idea when I overheard my 2-leggeds say they were going to get me fixed. Our car ran better after they got it fixed, and so did our fridge. It seemed like a good idea for me to get fixed. I figured I'd come home better than ever.

But it didn't turn out that way. I've never been the same since I got fixed. I lost my taste for staying out all night exploring and chasing after girl-cats. Believe me, there's such a thing as being TOO mellow.

Once I got fixed, all I wanted to do was eat and sleep.

But maybe that's not really so bad, after all, is it? Isn't that a cat's purpose in life, to eat and sleep and hang out with his 2-leggeds and make them happy?

Don't get fixed!

Fight it tooth and claw!

Spread the word! Put this bumper-sticker on your family car!

Rule #17

Just so it's clear:

Cats are purrfect, just the way we are.

But DOGS ALWAYS NEED FIXING!

The dog who lives next door is named Chester, but everybody always called him Chester Barker, because that's how he spent his life, barking and barking and barking.

Then his 2-leggeds got him fixed, and that made everything better. Now he doesn't come over and try to steal my plate any more. All he wants is to sit inside by the fireplace. Now that he's fixed, he's pretty likable. As dogs go, that is.

Rule #18

JUST SAY NO TO DRUGS!

<u>Especially</u> pills!

JUST SPIT THEM OUT!

But be very careful! Sneaky 2-leggeds may try to HIDE the pills in your food, or grind them up and mix them with your favorite taste treats, maybe even in your tuna soup.

Outsmart them. Just eat the good parts and spit out the rest. Show them who's boss!

Rule #19

Sick and hurting? That's when you deserve extra-special care!

Suppose you find yourself not up to par, maybe from eating a little too much, or maybe because you got into a little fight and came home achy and all scratched up.

Don't eat. Hard to believe, but this is a time when it's best not to eat. Just let nature take its course, flushing out all the bad stuff. Besides, when your 2-leggeds notice that you're not interested in food, they will pamper you in other ways.

Very important: Keep a count of the meals you missed. They are owed you, so you can catch them up later.

Tip: If you haven't learned to count, then just scratch a mark on the wood for each meal you miss.)

Tip: If they take you to the doctor's, don't get mad, just act scared. That will make them feel guilty, and they'll make it up to you later.

Rule #20

INSOMNIA!

A cat's worst nightmare!

You've probably heard the old saying, "A cat who's tired of sleeping and eating is tired of living."

Personally, I've always been ready to eat, and usually ready to sleep right afterwards.

But if you're like me, there are times after a hard day when I'm DOG-TIRED BUT SLEEP JUST WON'T COME!

MY SECRET REMEDIES FOR INSOMNIA

1   A bowl of warm milk before bed-time sets you off
on the right paw.   If your 2-leggeds like to have a cup of
warm milk at bed-time, then make it your business to
drop by the kitchen to spend some quality time with
them and have some milk for yourself.

2   There's another old saying: "Misery loves company."
If YOU can't sleep, then there's no reason why THEY
should sleep, either. Jump up on their bed, walk
around, work on a hair-ball, do whatever it takes to get
them up and going.

Chances are, once you've gotten them awake, they'll
head out to the kitchen for a snack. Go with them,
keep them company.

The family that midnight-snacks together sleeps better!

Rule #21

It's good to

THINK

Outside the box.

But always

GO

Inside the box!

Seems pretty obvious, but some cats

JUST DON'T GET IT!

Hey, Albert McThumbs, are you pawing attention?

This means YOU!

Rule #22

A Called Cat never comes.

(Not if he's smart, that is.)

A smart cat ignores the call the first time.

Sometimes he even hides ...

Until they make it worth his while!

<u>Rule #23</u>

Never hurry through a door.

For one thing, you don't know what's on the other side of that door. There's no point in rushing into trouble.

But pawsing at doors is more than just catly caution, it's a matter of style and dignity. Smart cats live at their own tempo, never allowing themselves to be drawn into the sense of urgency that drives our servers.

Suppose you're outside, and your providers open the door and call for you to come in. Do not jump! You're not their servant, they're yours, AND NEVER LET THEM FORGET THAT.

Otherwise, stop and think about it: do you really want to go in now? Wouldn't you rather have them come back and check on you every few minutes?

Wouldn't you really rather have them give you a special snack as a reward for coming in?

When you finally do decide to step inside, always paws for a nice stretch as you step across the threshold. S-T-R-E-E-E-T-C-H until every muscle is relaxed.

Then sniff-sniff-sniff so you have a sense of who's there, and what they have waiting for you. Then and only then complete your journey through the door.

The 2-leggeds will try to hurry you. Sometimes they'll complain that you're letting all the hot air out, other times that you're letting all the cold air in. Hot, cold, in, out — it's all very confusing. In any case, that's their problem, not yours.

Don't let yourself be rushed. Just ignore them. Take your time.

Rule #24

Exercise daily — in moderation.

Personally, I find taking my daily bath gives me all the exercise I need. It's a real streeeetch to reach waaaay down below the tummy. That leaves me nicely relaxed so I can snooooze.

Part Four
Managing Your People

Rule #25

2-leggeds are human beings.

We are feline beings.

The way I see it, we all have our places in life. 2-leggeds were put here to invent things like refrigerators and can openers so they can take better care of the 4-legged folks who live with them.

On the other paw, we 4-legged people were put here to bring meaning to their lives and give them something to get up in the morning for.

Seems to me, we're all here to scratch each other's backs and tummies. That's the way things work best.

Here's me—who else?—with my main 2-legged provider.

People say we look a lot alike. I guess that's because we're both big, powerfully-built guys with sort of the same hair color.

42

Rule #26

Don't expect too much of them.

After all, they're only human.

They're bigger than we are, they can open refrigerators and milk cartons and do lots of other useful tricks, but when you come down to it, they're only human.

That's really kind of sad, I think.

Compared to us cats, they have almost no sense of smell, they're blind in the dark, and they're practically deaf. The only way they can climb is with ladders, and they lack our ability to curl up and get comfortable anytime, anywhere.

Saddest of all, they don't know how to live. They're always running, keeping busy, never pausing for naps and contemplations.

All reasons why we feline beings need to take and keep control.

Rule #27

Always be the trainer,

Never the trainee.

Our providers think that because they're bigger that makes them smarter than us. That's silly, of course, but it's best to let them go on believing it. That way, we can manipulate them, and they never realize what's happening.

In other words, when there's "training" to be done, it should be we cats who do the training, NEVER the other way around. ("Training" is another word for manipulating.)

Here are a couple of case studies showing how we can twist things around so when they think they are training us, we are in fact training them, and they never catch on.

Case study #1: door training

When I moved south, my new main provider spent hours and hours on the porch just outside the door, plunking away at his computer. He'd try to make me come out and keep him company, but I didn't want that. Instead, I'd wait until I felt like going out, and then I'd flap the window curtains to signal him to open the door for me.

Once I was outside, I'd turn around and meow to be let back in, maybe have a sip of milk, then turn around again and flap the curtain to be let back out. Out and in, in and out until he got it down pat. Practice makes perfect.

Now, all I need to do is walk toward the door, pause, and look back over my shoulder at him. That's his signal to get up and open the door for me.

Case study #2: training them to provide welcome-back snacks

It's really important to eat before setting off on an outdoor adventure. You need lots of energy.

But it's even more important to have a bite as soon you come back in. That's something that 2-leggeds just can't seem to grasp. Without training, they'll open the door and let us in and then forget about us. Here's how to train them to follow through with the welcome-home plate you need.

First, go outdoors just before bedtime, then hide. Avoid your usual spots, because that's where they'll come looking when they're ready to go to bed. Maybe scoot under the car, or go next door and tuck yourself under some bushes. You want a place where they can't see you, but where you can watch them searching for you, calling your name, maybe even getting out the flashlights.

Then, stay there, no matter how tired or hungry you are, until they break out the food. Listen for them banging a spoon onto a can, or even running the electric can opener—the signals you know mean food.

Important : When you're hiding, don't snicker, don't even purr, or you'll give the game away!

THEN and only then saunter up to the door as usual. But caution: Make sure you actually see food on your plate before you step through the door, because they're going to slam it shut, fast, and then there's no going back.

Do this a few times, and you'll soon find they give you a snack every time you come home. They think they are training you to come when called, never realizing that you have trained them to make it worth your while to answer their call!

Rule #28

Meow softly.

(But keep your claws sharp, just in case.)

As a 27-pound Maine Coon, I'm a big guy, so I don't need a big voice. But, no matter, I have had to learn some tips on how to get through to my people when they are forgetful.

Level One: Basic reminders

Our first step is simply, Just be there. No matter how tired I am, I always snap alert when they come into the room around mealtimes. If you have a kind of eager, expectant look on your face, and stare at them and what they're eating, they'll usually get the point and serve you a share.

Level Two: Advanced reminders

Next on the scale is Speak up, loud and clear. Especially in the mornings before breakfast, it's helpful to yip out some impatient, indignant meows, to hurry them along.

Rule #29

A VISIBLE kitty

is a WELL-FED kitty.

So, Keep them Kompany in the Kitchen!

Important: while you wait, always look up at the cook with your big, adoring eyes. They can't resist!

His stage name is Mr. Blue-Eyes, but his friends and family know him as Pistol.

Rule #30

Help with the dishes!

Always lick your plate clean!

It's not just a NICE thing to do, it's a VERY SHREWD move, too. If you don't clean every morsel off your plate, your 2-leggeds might start thinking they've dished out too much, and cut back next time.

Remember, too, what our Momcats taught us, there are starving kitties all around the world, so it's important never to let any food go to waste!

Rule #31

When they come home at the end of the day,

MEET `EM,

GREET `EM, &

LEAD `EM . . .

. . . TO THE KITCHEN! WHERE ELSE?

MEET THEM. You'll be hungry and tired and upset at having been left all alone. No matter: you need to be waiting right by the door. If you're indoors, stand at the window where they can see you when they drive in.

Tip: You don't really need to stay in the window, just listen for the car and jump up so it looks as though you've been looking forward to their arrival for hours. (Be sure to rub the sleep out of your eyes so they don't catch on.)

Tip: If you're outdoors when they arrive home, run over to be with them as they climb out of the car. That makes them feel important — and generous.

GREET THEM. Rub up against their legs to show how much you love them and how glad you are to see them. Establish eye-contact. Meow, especially with a hungry or weak tone. Note: if they are wearing dark clothes they may try to pull away, out of fear that your fur will clash with their ensemble. But pay no attention: they secretly love your affectionizing them, and are happy to brush away a few hairs.

Rule #32

TIME

(whatever that is)

IS ON OUR SIDE!

So, be patient!

Out-wait them!

Wear them down!

Rule #33

Never forget:

YOU ARE THE CAT!

You take orders from

NOBODY!

Rule #34

Seize the power spot!

There are usually several power spots in the normal house, depending on the time of day.

Tip: The most important power spot, the one to control above all others, is the kitchen, especially before and during meals. When your 2-leggeds are cooking is definitely NOT the time to be out on the sofa, catching your ZZZs.

Keep your priorities straight: eat first, sleep later.

Tip: Other good power spots include the bed, as well as the most comfortable chairs in the living room.

Grab those spots, and you'll be not only comfy, but in control.

Tip: Still other power spots are places where the traffic flows come together, so you can keep your eye on what's happening. In my house, that means the hallway where the flows from the kitchen to the bedrooms meet those from the living room to the back porch. Choose a spot like that, and you'll be in the heart of all the action.

That way, if anybody heads down to the kitchen for a snack or cup of tea, you'll be the first to know, so be ready to dog their footsteps and claim your own snack, or maybe a nice bowl of milk.

If they try to make fun of you, maybe like calling you names like "The Hall Monitor," just shrug it off like you would a raindrop.

Here's one of my favorite pictures, me in my kitchen power spot., on my heated bed.

Notice the portraits of me on the wall. They were painted by some of my 2-legged lady admirers. What a great life I have!

Rule #35

Learn your name.

But answer to it

ONLY

when you're hungry.

Rule #36

Catch a mouse

INSIDE the house—

That makes you a <u>hero!</u>

SUPER-SPECIAL TOP-SECRET TIP: Win bonus points as a Rodent Control Expert by sneaking your trophies inside!

Here you see my Nellie doing that, and her 2-leggeds never caught on!

Part Five
New Places and Mew Friends

Rule #37

How to set up in a new territory

We cats love the comfort of knowing that our world is secure, and never get tired of revisiting our favorite spots. Once we settle into a home we never want to leave, and never want anything to change.

Unfortunately, our servers are not like that at all. They pick up and move, and drag us along with them.

I made the first big move of my life when my first provider got sick, and they shipped me south. I didn't like that at first. It was bad enough to be stuffed into a cage and carried. That offended my dignity.

But then we walked through the airport and I saw all those new people. I'd never realized there were so many 2-leggeds in the world, and every one of them looked different.

Then I saw that most of them smiled when they saw me, and some even wanted to come over and scratch my head. That was nice, so I didn't't bite them.

Then we got to my new home. It was in a place called Reston, and that sounded good. Then I heard the town's motto, "We're not dead, we're just Reston," and I knew it was going to be my kind of place. Reston or restin' — I liked the sound of that right from the start.

IF YOU MUST CHANGE HOMES – HERE ARE SOME TIPS TO EASE THE STRAIN

Stay close to home for the first few days in your new locale. This is very important, as your CPS (Cat Positioning System) needs those few days to adjust.

Use those early days in your new home to rest up from the journey. Pamper yourself. Travel is grueling.

Take your first strolls outside only after dark, as that's the time of day we're most in our feline element. Keep your nose open and sniff every bush and post so you get a sense of who and how many other cats live in the area.

Tip: Most "postings" are done by male cats, especially those lucky enough to have escaped being fixed. Some of them may be bullies, so stay out of their way until you know if they're big and mean.

Of course that wasn't anything I needed to worry about. If you're like me, 27 pounds of muscle, jaws and claws, then you need have no fear as you'll be Top Dog from the start.

As you roam, mark your path so you can find your way back home. Also, mark all around your place so other cats know you've arrived on the scene.

Marking your territory should come naturally, but just in case you've lived your whole life in an apartment, here's how: simply back up to markers like fenceposts, shrubs, doors, cars, sheds, or anything else, and spra-a-a-a-y.

61

Rule #38

Worried about the dogs in your new territory?
Just keep this in mind:

You can fool MOST of the people,

MOST of the time,

But you can ALWAYS fool a dog!

Rule #39

Make mew friends, and let them show you around.

One morning, not long after I moved into my new home, I was sitting out by our front door, digesting my breakfast and planning my day, when I heard a strange scratching sound coming up the fence.

Soon a furry gray head with two big green eyes popped over the top of the fence, and the rest of her followed, and that was how I met Kitty, the best friend I've ever had in my life. The best teacher, too.

We had a lot of hissing contests before Kitty and I got to know and like each other. But my provider helped by putting out an extra plate for her whenever she dropped by, and that smoothed things over. And she started dropping by more and more, and soon every day.

Kitty showed me around the neighborhood, and pointed out the houses where other cats lived, and where there were older 2-leggeds who were kind and generous to visiting felines.

Before long, we were hanging out together for hours at a time, a pack of two feline predators on the prowl -- a crafty Gray Tiger teaming up with the Mighty Orange Lion, the King of the Suburban Jungle.

On days when the weather wasn't so good, we'd go to Kitty's house, slipping in through the secret cat door, and spend a rainy afternoon snoozing and snacking.

One time her people came home early and caught me surveying the world from their bedroom window. I don't think they liked that.

But most of the time, after our prowls, and an afternoon nap, we'd lurk out by the garage when it was time for my guy to come home from work. Then we'd stalk him to the kitchen -- me in the front, Kitty behind, sometimes another feline friend bringing up the rear. It was slow-motion stalking, but nonetheless good practice for keeping our skills up to date.

In Reston, catnip Parties were a very big social event on warm sunny days. Other guys, like Spunky and the Tail-less Wonder and the Boxer, would crash the party.

That was okay, except that the Boxer always sniffed too much 'nip and then wanted to pick a fight with me. Some folks just never learn!

Kitty—my best friend, ever

We had lots of good times, then Kitty didn't come out to go roaming very much, and when she did show up, she was limping, and she looked skinny and not herself.

After a while, she stopped coming out at all, even though I was there waiting in the bushes where we met up at night when we could sneak out of the house. Night after night I waited, and she didn't show up.

Then I heard them say she was sick, and her people were taking her to the vet's. And I never saw her again.

I hope we're together again in all our next lifetimes!

66

Rule #40

Find your way

To a Kitty-Kat Kafe

Kitty had traveled all over everywhere with her family, and told me a secret, which I'll pass it on to you. The secret is that in every neighborhood, you can find the homes of kindly 2-leggeds who leave snacks for passing pussycats.

These places are kalled Kitty-Kat Kafes.

Don't be bashful. There's always plenty to eat at a Kafe, and the 2-leggeds are glad to see you, so make a point of learning where these places are, just in case you get caught away from home and feel weak from hunger. The Kafe is also the place to go for a bite if your own servers are late getting home.

A Kitty-Kat Kafe is also a good place to meet and talk shop with the other 4-leggeds in the neighborhood. The friends you make there can help you find your way to still other Kafes!

Rule #41

Join your local Free-Lunch Bunch.

Cats are not very sociable by nature, not at all like dogs, or like the Rotarians and Unitarians and bridge-players are among the 2-leggeds.

That's the way we are, and we don't want to change our nature.

But sometimes it pays to make the effort to build a network of friends of our own sort, so we can trade ideas and keep up with the local gossip.

So how do you make those contacts? Simple, just keep your eyes open (while you're awake, of course), and follow your nose.

Just use your common-scents, follow your nose to where things smell good, and chances are you'll meet other savvy kitties there. True, they may not be very welcoming at first, as we are a territorial bunch, but if you bring something to the party, you'll be accepted.

So what should you to bring to the party? Your own good ideas, or even bring some of my ideas from this book. (But if you, be sure to give me credit so those other folks will want their own copies!)

Tip: Or invite the gang back to your place to they can sample your folks' food. Then they'll HAVE to invite you next time!

Rule #42

If they leave a plate out, we will come.

It's very sad, but not every cat has a home where he's provided for by his own 2-leggeds.

On the other paw, not every cat wants to live with 2-leggeds. There are some cats who are free spirits and like to come and go as they please, and are willing to sacrifice the comforts of a warm bed and full bowl for their independence. (It's their choice, but a dumb move, in my opinion.)

But most cats without homes and providers are orphans -- homeless through no fault of their own. Maybe they got lost, or were thrown out by evil providers. (I've made it my private crusade to find homes for homeless orphan cats . . . but that's a story for another time.)

The fact is, even as you read this, there are cats lurking nearby, ready to pounce on any stray morsels of food.

Don't believe me? Just watch at the window some night when your 2-leggeds forget to bring in your plate. Stay awake, and you'll probably see a stranger, maybe even a whole posse of scruffy, skinny cats, drop by to scavenge those left-over morsels.

When you see that, shhh! Don't hiss, don't make a sound, lest your 2-leggeds go out and chase him away. Just sit there and watch him eat, and be thankful you're inside, warm and dry, with a full tummy and a nice bed waiting you.

By the way, that's Graycie in the picture here, and I have a really nice heart-warming story about Graycie still to come.

My point is, if they (our 2-leggeds) leave food out, we (our feline brothers and sisters) will come and clean it up.

That's a good thing, PROVIDED those cats don't get any ideas about moving in and taking over our places!

Rule #43

Chipmunks and birds are a lot more fun to watch than to eat.

Chipmunks are very interesting. Some of those little guys live in our back-yard, and each one is as different as one 2-legged person is from another. Every one of them has his own personality and habits.

Here are some tips on chipmunk watching.

Tip #1: Be Alert!

My very favorite 'munk is a fat little guy the 2-leggeds call Pavarotti because he wakes up in the morning and climbs up on the wood-pile as his stage, and then sings and sings, and that really starts the day off in a very nice way.

Alvin is another singing 'munk, but he's too lazy to serenade us for very long. He likes to follow squirrels, digging up the peanuts they hide. (Squirrels are interesting, but they're kind of dim. Not like chipmunks.)

Another chipmunk lives under our apple tree. Every so often, he pops his head up out of his hole, looks around, then ducks back under cover. For some reason, the 2-leggeds call him The Tank Commander.

Tip #2: Be Ready to Pounce! (Even though it's just pretend.)

On nice afternoons, Penthouse Pete appears on the ledge beneath the upstairs window. Sometimes he sings, but mostly he just lies up there in the sun, watching the world happening down below. He and I are a lot alike, I think. We could be really good friends, hanging out together. But he runs away whenever I go near him.

Fatso is the little guy who lives in the front. He doesn't sing, he just stands around and waits for the 2-leggeds to throw peanuts. He's a smart little guy: if they're slow to serve him, then he'll run back and forth, the way we cats make a point of walking past the refrigerator to give a hint that it's time to serve us.

Tip #3: Chipmunk watching is hard work, so take breaks. Nap as needed!

Part Six
Final Things

Rule #44

No matter what,

HOLD YOUR TAIL UP HIGH!

Don't let the little things get you down!

Rule #45

Stay on top of the news.

I love newspapers. Not for what's printed in them, of course, that's all just trash. What I like about newspapers is that they're comfy.

If your 2-leggeds are like mine, they read a section of the newspaper, then toss it in a pile on the floor.

Don't hesitate! Move in fast and plop onto that paper. Before very long, you'll find it's giving you a very warm, cozy feeling down below. There's something about a newspaper that makes it seem almost as warm as an electric blanket. Plop on a newspaper on top of a nice soft rug, and you're perfectly positioned for a really great snooze.

I really look forward to weekends. There's really nothing nicer on a rainy day than a long nap on a nice, thick Sunday paper.

Rule #46

Prepare now for your lives to come!

Sometimes, when time hangs heavy because I'm hungry or can't sleep, I ask myself what I'd do if I had this lifetime to live all over again.

It's a hard question.

Momcat used to tell us we have only nine lives, and need to live them wisely.

It's sad they took me away from her before I was old enough to understand what she meant about those nine lives.

Did she mean I might come back in my next life as a 2-legged person? I don't think I'd like that. It'd be nice to be tall enough to open the refrigerator on my own, or to pop open a can of food whenever I felt like it. But most 2-leggeds are just too busy-busy for my taste. They go away all day, doing who knows what, and even when they get home, they just don't plop down and take it easy.

Every time I open my eyes, Suzie, my food-preparer, is puttering here or there. If she's not cleaning the house, then she's out digging in the garden, or putting dishes away. That's not for me. Just keeping myself clean is more than I can handle. I can't see spending all that time cleaning a house when you could be sleeping.

Then there's Mikie, my other provider. At least he sits in one place for hours on end, but why does he punch that keyboard all day long? What does he see in that computer screen that can be as nice as a snooze and a dream?

But maybe we don't have a choice about coming back in that next life. Maybe if we're a bad cat in one lifetime, then in the next we're sent back as a 2-legged to learn a lesson!

The Big Question

But I'm rambling. The question is, What would I do if I had my life to live over? More to the point, How do I want to spend those eight more lives that I have waiting down the line?

No matter how many times I ask the question, in the end it all comes down to the same answer. If I had this lifetime to live over, I'd do it just about the same way as this time.

Let's face it: I've got it pretty good as it is.

I don't have to go out and chase mice for a living.

I don't have to get up in the morning and put on a necktie or high heels and go off to a job and try to stay awake all day.

I don't have a house to keep clean.

I have servers to fix my food and clean my litter-box, and I have people lined waiting to invite me to visit them on my vacations.

I have Mikie and Suzie to brush me and bring me special treats and snuggle up against at night.

What more could I ask for?

Why would I want to change it? Just let me have it like this forever, lifetime after lifetime

I'm in heaven in this lifetime!

Rule #47

Go toward the light.

Oops! I almost forgot: the bright spots on the rug show where the warm sunlight is streaming in, and that's the best place to settle down for an afternoon's nap.

This is Nellie glowing in the light. Who else?

Rule #48

If all else fails, TAKE A NAP!

Here they caught me napping on my heated bed, next to the radiator—that's what works best for me.

By the way, this shows my Lion's Cut fur style for summer. I bet you wish you had a mane like mine!

Final Rule

Share with the homeless and hungry— that could be you in your next lifetime!

It's important to bear in mind that we cats have nine lifetimes. (In case you're not good on numbers and counting, that's almost as many claws as you have on your front paws.)

We don't know what those lifetimes to come will hold for us, but maybe we can do ourselves (and other cats) a big favor by sending good things forward.

Some say it's setting up good Cat-arma, which is like Karma is for 2-leggeds.

Here's my pal Al stepping aside to let poor homeless Graycie have a bite.

Al himself was homeless all one cold winter, so he knows what it's like!

Now Graycie has found a wonderful home with the loves of her life both a very special 4-legged guy, and 2-leggeds, and all she wants to eat, and soft, warm places to sleep summer and winter!

Don't you love stories with happy endings?

Other Important Stuff

PS #1

You've GOT it, so FLAUNT it!

Use your natural cat-cutes!

Charm them!

You've got to paw it to Shadow, he's a real charmer!

PS #2

Love your people.

But keep an eye on them, just in case.

This is Sweet Pea, a master of undercover observation.

PS #3

Be exuberant! Be joyous! Jump for joy!

This is my little cousin, Charlotte. Sometimes when my person was away, I'd go and stay with her and her twin sister, and we'd have nice dinners together.

Looking back, I wonder if maybe I ate more than my share of those dinners.

But, on the other paw, she was practicing to be a catrobat, and did a

lot of climbing and jumping, so needed to stay really lean and agile. Or was it to be a ballerinacat? I can't remember.

So I guess I don't have to feel bad if I ate a little more than my share: she was probably watching her diet, anyway.

PS #4

Ask smart questions.

Peek-a-Boo's smart question is,

   "What happens if I step through the Looking Glass?"

Well, I don't know the answer to that question. Can anycatbody out there help? Write me at www.catselfhelp.com

Appendix

Checklist on the care and feeding of healthy, full-bodied cats.

Certain 2-leggeds who call themselves "experts" claim that food should be served for cats only twice each day, and left out for not more than a half hour.

---Which only shows how little human beings really know about the feline beings with whom they are blessed!

If that's such a good idea, then why don't 2-leggeds try it for themselves? The ones I know eat more times every day than I have whiskers!

 If cats are to grow up big and strong – and stay that way – then they should be fed according to the following schedule. This feeding schedule is your catstitutional right.

Cut these pages out and stick them on the door of your family's refrigerator, where the 2-leggeds can't help but be reminded every time they go to grab food for themselves!

Breakfast, served at dawn, should be ample, ready as soon as the cat awakens. Delaying this meal creates further anxiety in a cat already worried about whether the family has died overnight, leaving him or her an orphan.

Second breakfast should be served about one to two hours after the initial breakfast. Though it can be slightly smaller in quantity than the first, it should offer a varied taste from the first. (Note: Second breakfast should not be confused with a "second helping" of breakfast itself, which is a matter of course.)

Mid-morning tea-time. While cats avoid tea and other stimulants, this is an appropriate time for a few tasty morsels of leftover ham or cheese while your two-legged is filling up on tea; that will ensure that you have a full tummy, so you can nap soundly in getting rested up for lunch.

Lunch. This is the most important meal of the cat's mid-day, and should be both ample and tasty. Caring servers never think of eating until they have made sure their resident cat has had enough. Again, second-helpings should be given as soon as the plate is clean.

"4-sies," your afternoon pick-me-up. Not only is this a good time to socialize with your house-mates and other friends, but some gentle exercise is helpful at this time of the day. (Walking to the kitchen from your nap-spot is sufficient exercise.) Low blood sugar from an empty stomach can make cats cranky and sluggish.

Dinner. Other than breakfast, there is no more important meal for the cat's well-being. But 2-leggeds should not expect the cat to sit down and eat dinner with the rest of the family. Rather, cats are solitary creatures, and should be served their meals first. If they then want to join in and also share the family's meat or fish dish they will so indicate.

"Niner" snack. Many cats need an energy-boosting snack around nine each evening. I personally pass this up nowadays, but cats who like to take an extended stroll should be well-nourished before they venture out.

Bedtime snack. This is a way of showing love to the little friend who shares the home and brightens the days of the two-leggeds. Cats need sleep, yet cats cannot sleep on empty stomachs.

Middle-of-the-night snack (if desired). Feline insomnia is a very cruel yet easily-cured condition. If I wake up hungry, I just can't get back to sleep. But if I'm given a little something to eat around three or four in the morning, I can usually sleep right through till first light, which is one of my favorite times of the day, as I can see a nice big breakfast coming across the sky toward me with the approaching dawn.

Want more copies of my wonderful book to send to your feline friends?

Want to send a review and tell the world how my advice has changed your life, and all of your lives to come?

Here's the link:

http://www.amazon.com/Eat-Well-Get-Lots-Rest/dp/06158066 35/

OTHER BOOKS BY MICHAEL MCGAULLEY

(Wolfie's editor and main food-server)

These are available in both e-book and printed versions

TECHNOTHRILLERS and NOVELS

A REMEDY FOR DEATH–Playing God with body, soul, and bio-tech

THE GRAIL CONSPIRACIES—A technothriller exploring deeper human possibilities

JOINING MIRACLES—Navigating the seas of latent possibility & synchronicity

CAREER SELF-HELP

HOW TO ASK THE SMART QUESTIONS FOR WINNING THE GAMES OF BUSINESS & LIFE

SALES HOW-TO

SELLING 101: CONSULTATIVE SELLING SKILLS

SALES TRAINING TUTORIALS: Small business sales how-to series

SALES PRESENTATIONS & DEMONSTRATIONS

Legal and copyright notices continued from the front of this book

24248042R00056

Made in the USA
Lexington, KY
11 July 2013